Jesus Said, "I Will Build My Church"

DON FAIX

authorHOUSE®

AuthorHouse™
1663 Liberty Drive
Bloomington, IN 47403
www.authorhouse.com
Phone: 833-262-8899

Published by AuthorHouse 09/22/2021

ISBN: 978-1-6655-3922-7 (sc)
ISBN: 978-1-6655-3921-0 (e)

Print information available on the last page.

Scripture taken from the King James Version of the Bible.

This book is printed on acid-free paper.

CONTENTS

CHAPTER 1

The Concept of Build

The primary focus of this book is on Jesus Christ and the concept of 'BUILD.' We are talking about building the church, not a building but a spiritual house. So let's start at the beginning, where Christ utters these words, "And Jesus answered and said unto him, "Blessed art thou, Simon Barjona: for flesh and blood hath not revealed it unto thee, but my Father which is in heaven. And I say also unto thee, That thou art Peter, and upon this rock I will build my church; and the gates of hell shall not prevail against it. And I will give unto thee the keys of the kingdom: and whatsoever thou shalt bind on earth shall be bound in heaven: and whatsoever thou shalt loose on earth shall be loosed in heaven." Mt.16:17-19.

Here our Lord speaks of the concept of 'building' in relationship to the church. This should lead every Christian to ask a simple question: "How did Jesus Christ intend every local church to be built?"

The Lord has blessed me, has given me opportunity

to speak to hundreds of pastors on this subject of 'build' – though it apparently escaped from their thinking. Yet we read in 1Cor.3:9-10, "For we are labourers together with God: ye are God's husbandry, ye are God's building. According to the grace of God which is given unto me, as a wise masterbuilder, I have laid the foundation, and another buildeth thereon. But let every man take heed how he buildeth thereupon."

Christians are exhorted to be careful how they build God's building.

The Body of Christ needs to be looking at the church through the lens of 'build.' In our passage from Mt.16:17-19 there are three particular important points. One is the concept of build. The second is, 'to prevail.' Will YOUR church prevail? Will it be around in the years to come? That's for another chapter.

The third point has to do with the kingdom of God.

This would be a good place to briefly discuss the purpose for the church. Jesus said he would build the church. Why? The church serves in many capacities but its primary function is to advance the kingdom of God. Jesus promised us power to be witnesses, to go forth and preach the gospel, to heal the sick and cast out demons, to confront the works of the devil – so that souls would be saved. Somewhere along the road, churches have put aside this great commission.

Many a church is filled with those claiming to be saved. They raise their hands in worship, say 'Lord, Lord,' yet do not do as Jesus says, who prophesy, drive out demons and do miracles in his name, and yet the Lord will say to them, as he did in Mt.7:21-23, "I never knew you: depart from me, ye that work iniquity."

We cannot get around the simple fact that the ability for the church to prevail and advance the kingdom of God are solely based on *how it is built*. That's why the concept of 'build' is so important.

I will present here in this text ten biblical principles for building a church. For some thirty years I have traveled by the grace of God to many a church of all denominations and non-denominational, teaching on the subject of build. The startling reality is that every church where I presented this seminar agreed that these are the basic biblical principles in building a church, and also admitted they were doing at most two of the ten – though the principles of building are not complicated.

Let me give you an example of building a house which we can all relate to. Suppose I listed the ten most basic parts of building a house, let's say: the walls, roof, flooring, windows, doors, electric, plumbing, heating and air, skilled craftsmen, craftsmen in every trade. Now you get to pick any two! Would you want to live in such a house? Would you say for the most part it is uninhabitable?

Of course it is! Well, these are the churches we are building today. They are close to being in ruins. Now you might say, "That's not our church." I can just about assure you that your church is no different. As we go through the ten principles of building a church, I hope they will bring to you a conviction to look more closely at this concept of build.

CHAPTER 2

Will Your Church Prevail?

Churches are crumbling all around us. Will your church be nothing but a statistic in 100 years or will it be thriving as a beacon of light to the lost? Many a Christian just does not care. As it says in 2Tim.3:1-5, "In the last days perilous times shall come." The passage goes on to say that professing Christians will be lovers of pleasure more than lovers of God, having a form of godliness but denying the power thereof. Are your pews filled with such folks?

In Revelation, chapters 2 and 3, the Lord gives a message to seven churches. To some of the seven he gives a stark warning. Let's look at some of the charges the Lord brought against them.

To the church at Ephesus he said they had left their first love, so now should go back and do their first works. By this point in time, this was most likely a second generation of believers. Had their devotion to Christ and the preaching of the gospel waned to such a point where Jesus now threatened to remove his presence if they did not repent?

To the church at Sardis, Jesus said they hung on to a reputation of being alive but were actually spiritually dead and their works not complete. As we talk here about sharing the gospel, let's remember that Jesus warned that he would come as a thief if they did not repent. And to the church at Laodicea he said he was not happy with their works either. He considered them lukewarm (he said) and warned them that if they did not repent he would spew them out of his mouth.

Could any of these churches be a reflection of your church? You say, "Of course not."

To this the Lord replies, "Because thou sayest, I am rich and increased with goods, and have need of nothing; and knowest not that thou art wretched, and miserable, and poor, and blind, and naked:" Rev.3:17.

Based on my observations of many churches, I believe that most have not a clue of the spiritual state they are in. Maybe they just don't care. Every one of the sins noted by the Lord (in these letters in Revelation) *are due to not building the church according to the Word of God.*

I cannot over-estimate the importance of this concept of 'build.'

To those who do care, and those who desire to prevail, and those who are able to hear what the spirit of the Lord is saying to the churches, I say, "Wake up!"

Chapter 3

Man's Ways of Building

As I began to study the concept of building the church, the Lord caused me to ask a simple question, "What had already been built in the Old Testament?"

Well, that wasn't too difficult: Noah's ark, the tabernacle and the temple. By studying the building of these three, I hoped to uncover the ways in which God builds. We will get to that soon.

There was also a fourth structure built, the city and tower of Babel.

This is recorded in Genesis chapter 11:1-8. "And the whole earth was of one language, and of one speech. And it came to pass, as they journeyed from the east, that they found a plain in the land of Shinar; and they dwelt there. And they said one to another, Go to, let us make brick, and burn them thoroughly. And they had brick for stone, and slime had they for mortar. And they said, 'Go to, let us build us a city and a tower, whose top may reach unto heaven; and let us make us a name, lest we be scattered abroad upon the face of the whole earth.' And the Lord came down to see the city and the tower, which the children of men had builded. And the Lord said, Behold, the people is one, and they have all one language; and this they begin to do: and now nothing will be restrained from them, which they have imagined to do. Go to, let us go down, and there confound their language, that they may not understand one another's speech. So the Lord scattered them abroad from thence upon the face of all the earth: and they left off to build the city."

Let's take a moment to see if we can learn anything from these verses. In verse 4 we read, "…..let us build us a city and a tower, whose top may reach unto heaven; and let us make us a name ……"

Scripture says this city and tower of Babel were built by man and for man – to make a name for man!

Oh! they thought. *'What a colossal achievement if we can build this tower all the way up to heaven. Surely by building such an edifice we will become famous.'*

They left God completely out of the picture. They were in open rebellion against the Lord who in Gen.9:1 commanded them to go forth and replenish the earth.

God was ill-pleased with their work. So the Lord scattered them and the building came to ruins. So what does this have to do with today's church?

I share with you here what I believe are two major problems facing the modern church.

One is *the physical building.* It has become a yoke around

the necks of many churches...the mortgage, upkeep, and payroll. It requires a lot of money.

Second point is *competition*. The sheer number of churches leaves churches fighting and contending for parishioners. The need for money and parishioners has caused many churches to go down a dark path for which there are no biblical grounds. This is the way of Babel.

These are incorporating the ways of the world to increase their membership *for the money*. Yes, its all about money. And God is left out.

You might say, "God hasn't been left out. We use the Bible. The Lord is doing great things here." But I say, we are not moved by sight but by faith – faith in the scriptures and the Son of God. If you have left out eight of ten principles in building your church, then your church is in ruins. God's Word does not lie. By now I hope you are getting the point in all this.

I'm going to cite one example: the Seeker Sensitive movement. Why? Because as many as 80-90% of all churches are employing it's MO. To briefly summarize, with the Seeker Sensitive movement the thinking goes like this: How can we make our church attractive to those seeking God so they will attend our church and hopefully in time get saved.

Of particular focus are the youth. As you have probably noticed the music has changed. We've gone from the hymns, to contemporary music, to bands, to loud rock music with fog affects and strobe lighting. We have jobs posted for 'pastors of art' who can make all this happen.

We train people to greet, at least three times – to make sure everyone is welcomed. And we make sure the website is set up so folks can pay their tithes online. Yes, make sure we get the money. And let's tame down the preaching – lest we offend anyone. Oh, and by the way, if you want to get saved just raise your hand where you are, repeat these words, and NOW YOU ARE SAVED.

Well, you get the picture. It's all about numbers and church growth and dollars.

Most church members have their heads in the sand. They have no clue to whether this is of the Lord. All they see is a growing church that's paying its bills – with a coffee shop to perk them up.

But is it Biblical?

Here's a verse from Rm.3:11. "There is none that understandeth, there is none that seeketh after God." Clearly God's Word says there is no one who seeks after God. The whole Seeker Sensitive movement is based on a godless principle.

And then from 1Cor.3:6-7, "I have planted, Apollo's watered; but God gave the increase. So then neither he that planteth any thing, neither he that watereth; but God that giveth the increase."

We can apply the latest techniques and demographics to grow in numbers those who attend church – but only the Lord can add to the church those who are getting saved.

Sadly, these worldly tactics *appear to work,* whether the people are saved or not, or become real disciples. These concerns appear to be of little consequence – for the bills are paid and church leaders are making a name for themselves.

Yes, they say, let us build us a church and make us a name for ourselves.

CHAPTER 4

A Prophetic Word from
the Book of Haggai

Almost everything that has been discussed so far can be summed up from a word the Lord gave to the prophet Haggai. This is a powerful passage that deals dramatically with the concept of build.

Haggai 1:1–12 *"In the second year of Darius the king, in the sixth month, in the first day of the month, came the word of the Lord by Haggai the prophet unto Zerubbabel the son of Shealtiel, governor of Judah, and to Joshua the son of Josedech, the high priest, saying,*

Thus speaketh the Lord of hosts, saying, This people say, The time is not yet come, the time that the Lord's house should be built.

Then came the word of the Lord by Haggai the prophet, saying,

Is it time for you, O ye, to dwell in your ceiled houses, and this house lie waste?

Now therefore thus saith the Lord of hosts; Consider your ways.

Ye have sown much, and bring in little; ye eat, but ye have not enough; ye drink, but ye are not filled with drink; ye clothe you, but there is none warm; and he that earneth wages to put it into a bag with holes.

Thus saith the Lord of hosts; Consider your ways.

Go up to the mountain, and bring wood, and build the house; and I will take pleasure in it, and I will be glorified, saith the Lord.

Ye looked for much, and, lo, it came to little; and when ye brought it home, I did blow upon it. Why? Saith the Lord of hosts. Because of mine house that is waste, and ye run every man unto his own house.

Therefore the heaven over you is stayed with dew, and the earth is stayed from her fruit.

And I called for a drought upon the land, and upon the mountains, and upon the corn, and upon the new wine, and upon the oil, and upon that which the ground bringeth forth, and upon men, and upon cattle, and upon all the labour of the hands.

Then Zerubbabel the son of Shealtiel, and Joshua the son of Josedech, the high priest, with all the remnant of the people, obeyed the voice of the Lord their God, and the words of Haggai the prophet, as the Lord their God had sent him, and people did fear before the Lord."

God's people were busy with their own concerns while the house of God was in ruins. so God spoke, said they were to consider their ways, realizing that all their toil had amounted to little —because they were putting their money into a bag with holes in it.

They were to BUILD the house of God. Why? So that the Lord could take pleasure in it and be glorified.

So let me say this: in these days we seem to get so

excited about worship – yet give little thought or regard to the building of His church. We pray, hold revival meetings, and so forth, always expecting much – which turns out to be little. Why?

Because the Lord blows it away. And why does he blow it away? Because his house is laid waste. It is the Lord who is calling for a drought on the labor of our hands.

Wake up, church! We are fighting against God!

Now to our next chapter, which leads the way to discovering ten basic principles in building a church.

CHAPTER 5

God's Ways of Building

I asked the question, "How did Jesus intend the local church to be built?"

And the Lord prompted me to ask another question: "What was built in the Old Testament?"

There are three things that the Lord had a part in building: Noah's Ark, the Tabernacle, and the Temple. We are looking for the mind of God as he builds. Were there any mannerisms, plans, methods, fashion or pattern after which the Lord built?

Noah's Ark

The building of Noah's Ark is described in Gen.6:13–16: "And God said unto Noah, the end of all flesh is come before me; for the earth is filled with violence through them; and, behold, I shall destroy them with the earth. Make thee an ark of gopher wood; rooms shalt thou make in the ark, and shall pitch it within and without with pitch. And this is the fashion which thou shalt make it of: The length of the ark shall be three hundred cubits, the breadth of it fifty cubits, and the height of it thirty cubits. A window shalt thou make to the ark, and in a cubit shalt thou finish it above; and the door of the ark shalt thou set in the side thereof; with lower, second, and third stories shalt thou make it."

And then verse 22, "Thus did Noah: according to all that God commanded him, so did he."

Verse 15a reads, "And this is the fashion which thou shalt make it of." Very simply, the Lord gave to Noah explicit instructions in the building of the Ark. And from verse 22, we see that Noah completely followed those instructions.

The Tabernacle

In Exodus 25:8-9 we read concerning the building of the tabernacle, "And let them make me a sanctuary; that I may dwell among them. According to all that I shew thee, after the pattern of the tabernacle, and the pattern of all the instruments thereof, even so shall ye make it." Again, as in the building of the Ark. a pattern after which to build the Tabernacle was given by the Lord.

This pattern that was shown to Moses was to be followed exactly. The reason for following these specifications precisely was that the Lord was to come down and dwell among them. The same is true of the church today.

The only thing that makes the church unique and important is that it is a place where the Holy Spirit dwells in every believer.

Reading on in chapter 25 to the end of Exodus, we see the great care that was taken in building every small detail of the Tabernacle. Moses may well have not have understood why each and every fabric in the building of the Tabernacle was designed that way, but we read over and over again in chapter 40 that everything was built "as the Lord commanded him."

Some of the last verses in Exodus are very significant. Ex. 40:33b-35, "So Moses finished the work. Then a cloud covered the tent of the congregation, and the glory of the Lord filled the tabernacle. And Moses was not able to enter into the tent of the congregation because the cloud covered thereon, and the glory of the Lord filled the tabernacle."

It was not until Moses finished the work that the cloud covered the Tent of Meeting, and the glory of the Lord filled the Tabernacle.

The Temple.

Now let's look at the building of the Temple. I Chron. 28:10-12, "Take heed now; for the Lord has chosen thee to build an house for the sanctuary; be strong, and do it. Then David gave to Solomon his son the pattern of the porch, and of the houses thereof, and of the treasuries thereof, and of the upper chambers thereof, and of the inner parlours thereof, and of the place of the mercy seat. And the pattern of all that he had by the spirit, of the treasuries of the house of God, of the courts of the house of the Lord, and of all the chambers round about, and of the treasuries of the dedicated things:"

Again, the Lord provided the 'pattern' to build the temple. We see this word pattern or fashion used by the Lord in describing how the Ark, the Tabernacle and the temple were to be built. The people were simply responsible for following God's instructions.

As we read about the construction of the tabernacle we find some other ways in which our Lord was involved in building.

For example, in Ex. 35:30-36: "And Moses said unto the children of Israel, See, The Lord hath called by name Bezaleel the son of Uri, the son of Hur, of the tribe of Judah;

And he hath filled him with the spirit of God, in wisdom, in understanding, and in knowledge, and in all manner of workmanship;

And to devise curious works, to work in gold, and in silver, and in brass, And in the cutting of stones, to set them, and in carving of wood, to make any manner of cunning work.

And he hath put in his heart that he may teach, both he, and Aholiab, the son of Ahisamach, of the tribe of Dan.

Them hath he filled with wisdom of heart, to work all manner of work, of the engraver, and of the cunning workman, and of the embroiderer, in blue, and in purple, in scarlet, and in fine linen, and of the weaver, even of them that do any work, and of those that devise cunning work.

Then wrought Bezaleel and Aholiab, and every wise hearted man, in whom the Lord put wisdom and understanding to know how to work all manner of work for the service of the sanctuary, according to all that the Lord had commanded."

The Lord chose Bezalel, Oholiab, and others in the construction of the sanctuary. It was the Lord who filled them with the Spirit of God and with the skill, ability and knowledge to make everything. He also gave to Bezalel and Oholiab the ability to teach others.

Where God was going to come down and dwell, not only did he provide the plans and pattern and architecture in every detail – he also enabled and empowered man to accomplish the work.

From the reports of the building of Noah's Ark, the Tabernacle, and the Temple, we find a summary of the ways of our Lord in building.

1.   God provides the pattern.
2.   God provides every detail needed in construction.
3.   God provides the builders.
4.   Obedience is required in every detail of building.
5.   Upon completion of the work the full glory of the Lord manifests.

This study begs us to ask two more questions concerning the church today:

What is the pattern for the church? And who are the builders of the church?

I still remember my excitement as I pondered these questions and began to search the New Testament for the answers.

Chapter 6

The Pattern

We started with the concept of build that led us to asking ourselves the question, "How did Jesus intend the local church to be built?" This in turn led us to the building of Noah's Ark, the Tabernacle and the Temple.

We discovered two main ways in which the Lord builds: the Lord provides the pattern, and the Lord provides the builders. In essence, our Lord provides everything. Would it not be reasonable then to expect the Lord to provide us a pattern to follow in building the church? And would we not also expect him to provide the builders? Why, of course! We need a scripture. We are looking for a specific passage of scripture as our pattern for the church. I remember scouring the New Testament in my excitement as I searched, and after a few months I found an answer.

Eph. 2:19-22: "Now therefore ye are no more strangers and foreigners, but fellow-citizens with the saints, and of the household of God; And are built upon the foundation of the apostles and prophets, Jesus Christ himself the chief corner stone; In whom all the building fitly framed together groweth unto an holy temple in the Lord: In whom ye also are builded together for an habitation of God through the Spirit."

These verses are so simple yet so profound.

According to it there are just three significant parts in building the church: the cornerstone, the foundation, and that which is built on the foundation.

The first stone laid in those days was the cornerstone from which the rest of the foundation was constructed. So our first stone to lay in building a church is Jesus Christ – for it is He upon which everything hinges.

The rest of the foundation built is also Jesus Christ – which we will see shortly.

Once the foundation is laid others can then build upon it. The Apostle Paul supports this concept from the earlier scripture we read, 1Cor.3:10, "According to the grace of God which is given unto me, as a wise masterbuilder, I have laid the foundation, and another buildeth thereon. But let every man take heed how he buildeth thereupon."

Another scripture we need to turn to is Lk. 6:46-49, "And why call ye me, Lord, Lord, and do not the things which I say? Whosoever cometh to me, and heareth my sayings, and doeth them, I will shew you to whom he is like: He is like a man which built an house, and digged deep, and laid the foundation on a rock: and when the flood arose, the stream beat vehemently upon that house, and could not shake it: for it was founded upon a rock. But he that heareth, and doeth not, is like a man that without a foundation built an house upon the earth; against which the stream did beat vehemently, and immediately it fell; and the ruin of that house was great."

Notice the results when a foundation was not laid: when the storms came the house collapsed and was completely destroyed.

Could this be the reason why many profess Christ but fall short of salvation? Is this why when troubles and persecution arise many turn away from the church? Is this why many in the church are still on milk and rarely read the Bible? Is this why there is such a lack of what I call real disciples who have forsaken all to follow Jesus? Is it because they are missing a solid foundation?

Many pastors and church leaders will argue, "We preach Jesus Christ." They'll quote 1 Cor. 3:10, referenced above, and say Paul already laid the foundation. But here Paul is talking specifically about the church at Corinth. He went on to lay other foundations. Just as every house and building needs a solid foundation, so does every Christian and every local church.

We need to go further and find out more clearly what it means to lay a foundation. So I continued my questioning of the Lord, "Lord, how do we lay a foundation in the church?" This whole discussion on laying a foundation took me 6 months because it was new to me and I wanted to make sure I got it right. The answer comes in the form of laying stone after stone, brick after brick, until the foundation is complete. We begin with the chief cornerstone, Jesus Christ. It must all stem from Jesus.

Let's read 1 Cor. 15:1-4, "Moreover, brethren, I declare unto you the gospel which I preached unto you, which also ye have received, and wherein ye stand; By which also are ye saved, if ye keep in memory what I preached unto you, unless ye have believed in vain. For I delivered unto you first of all that which I also received, how that Christ died for our sins according to the scriptures; And that he was buried, and that he rose again the third day according to the scriptures: …"

Wherever the apostle Paul went he first preached the gospel by which we are saved. Our salvation is based on the death and resurrection of Jesus Christ. No more and no less. Obviously this then becomes our first stone to be laid after Christ. We see Paul's zeal in preaching this from 1 Cor. 2:2, "For I determined not to know any thing among you, save Jesus Christ, and him crucified."

Now let's go to Hebrews 6:1-2. "Therefore leaving the principles of the doctrine of Christ, let us go unto perfection; not laying again the foundation of repentance from dead works, and of faith toward God, of the doctrine of baptisms, and of laying on of hands, and of the resurrection of the dead, and of eternal judgment."

Our next stone to be laid in the foundation are the elementary teachings about Christ. Don't miss the words 'about Christ'. These elementary teachings – repentance, faith, instruction about baptisms, the resurrection of the dead and eternal judgment – are a further explanation of this gospel of salvation.

Without getting too deep into this, I'll share just a few more stones to be laid in no specific order.

Here are Jesus's first words to his disciples in Mt. 4:19, "Follow me, and I will make you fishers of men." From the beginning, a Christian needs to understand what he or she is getting into. *It is the winning of souls.*

Jesus's first teaching is the Sermon on the Mount in Matthew 5-7. Interestingly this begins with the Beatitudes. Our attitude must be right with God if we are to be effective disciples.

Since we are to imitate Christ, we must look at what he did and what he taught. Acts 1:1, "The former treatise have I made, O Theophilus, of all that Jesus began both to do and teach."

Today the Church is all over the place in what it teaches. But do the people have a foundation in their life? Let me share a brief story from my past experiences. The Lord has been very gracious in his dealing with me. From the moment I got saved there were two great desires in me, to study the scriptures, and preach the gospel. In subsequent years the Lord opened many doors in churches for me to preach the gospel and teach on evangelism. During the seminars on evangelism I always ask the following two questions.

First, "If you were to die today do you know for sure you would go to heaven?"

And second, "What are you trusting in to get to heaven?"

I ask these questions in various ways to make sure the ones hearing grasp what it is I'm asking. Only about 10% of those who respond answer both questions correctly. I find the same in witnessing door to door. Almost 90% of the people I've visited going door to door attend church, yet only 10% get those questions right – and I've knocked on thousands of doors, which makes for an alarming statistic!

What's the reason for this? The reason is that the foundation has not been properly laid. These are the people sitting in your pews who have all heard the message of salvation but have not fully understood nor grasped this gospel message to where they can come to repentance and faith in Christ, and therefore, are likely not saved. Since they lack the indwelling of the Holy Spirit, all their labor is in vain and of no value in building the church.

We know that the apostle Paul spent a lot of time laying a foundation, six months, a year or two or more. It wasn't some casual undertaking. Paul realized that everything that happened in the life of a new convert rested on this foundation. Paul taught these same principles in every church – that was his gifting, and then he moved on.

In this section we have looked at two of the ten principles of building a church. The first is laying a foundation (discussed in some length). The second principle in building a church is building upon the foundation. Before we're finished, we will see how all ten principles of building a church fit together.

The question to ask is, 'Why are we today not laying a proper foundation?' We shall see as we try to answer our second question — '*Who are* the builders of the church?

CHAPTER 7

Who are the Builders of the Church?

What's paramount here is to understand that Jesus is a builder. It is this concept of 'build" we need to concentrate on – and get into our spirit.

The second point we learned from studying the biblical principles of building the church is that *God provides the builders*. So who are the builders of the church?"

The question leads us to a passage many Christians are familiar with.

Eph.4:7-16, "But unto everyone of us is given grace according to the measure of the gift of Christ. Wherefore he saith, When he ascended up on high, he led captivity captive, and gave gifts unto men. (Now that he ascended, what is it but that he also descended first into the lower parts of the earth? He that descended is the same also that ascended up far above all heavens, that he might fill all things.) And he gave some, apostles; and some, prophets; and some, evangelists; and some, pastors and teachers; For the perfecting of the saints, for the word of the ministry, for the edifying of the body of Christ: Till we all come in the unity of the faith, and of the knowledge of the Son of God, unto a perfect man, unto the measure of the stature of the fullness of Christ; That we henceforth be no more children, tossed to and fro, and carried about with every wind of doctrine, by the sleight of men, and cunning craftiness, whereby they lie in wait to deceive; But speaking the truth in love, may grow up into him in all things, which is the head, even Christ: From whom the whole body fitly joined together and compacted by that which every joint supplieth, according to the effectual working in the measure of every part, maketh increase of the body unto the edifying of itself in love."

In essence this text says that when Christ ascended he gave gifts to men, apostles, prophets, evangelists, pastors and teachers, to equip the saints for the work of the ministry, to build up the body of Christ. These apostles, prophets, evangelists, pastors and teachers are to build. These gifts were actually men as opposed to gifts of the Holy Spirit and they are referred to in some circles as the 5-fold ministry.

To understand how important these men are, we must understand that there are just three major gifts the Lord has given believers: the gift of eternal life, the Holy Spirit, and these gifted men. We should not take them lightly.

The third principle in building a church is the builders – apostles, prophets, evangelists, pastors and teachers. Why do we need all five?

I have learned that the answer to so many questions comes back to Jesus. The scriptures tell us Jesus was an apostle, a prophet, a teacher, and a shepherd (pastor).

You do the study. It does not say he was an evangelist, but surely he came to preach the good news and save the lost. Therefore Jesus had what we would refer to as a 5-fold ministry. Jesus is the full and total expression of all ministries. All elements of his ministry must become manifest in believers in order for the church to become fully equipped and built up.

This 5-fold ministry is an extension of Jesus Christ. We would be naïve to think that all these same gifts are not for today. What we are looking at here is God's plan for building the church. It is our job to obey and utilize this 5-fold ministry.

The passage from Ephesians is parallel to what we read earlier in Exodus – about the builders of the tabernacle. Therefore, for example, the apostles have been called by God and given skill, ability and knowledge to carry out the construction of the sanctuary, the church. Unless you have been chosen by the Lord as an apostle there is nothing you can do to replicate this gift.

We notice that the apostle Paul may have functioned in various roles of the 5-fold ministry, but he was clearly called an apostle -- thus there is separation of these gifts, and no one has two callings.

What's important to understand here is that all five roles

are needed to construct and/or build up the body of Christ – your local church.

Let me give you an example. If you were to construct a house, which house would you rather live in? The house built by a plumber, or the house built by a mason, carpenter, plumber, electrician and roofer? We have today what I call a pastoral-oriented church, for it is built almost exclusively by pastors. This can become a lopsided view as we take on solely the view of the pastor – instead of the entirety of Jesus Christ.

The result? People suffer. They are not properly equipped to do the work of ministry – the preaching of the gospel, the healing of the sick, the deliverance from demons. This is what the apostles were equipped to do – the seventy that Jesus sent out, as well as the disciples we read about in Acts.

In this current time Christians are more often asked and taught to serve by getting involved in child care, greeting, ushering, the choir, church repairs, passing out flyers, and so on. None of these are noted in the Bible and none of these build up the church spiritually – and then we wonder why Christians never mature as real disciples of Christ. Our churches today are organized by man-made patterns, laid down upon the traditions of men. Most Christians and most pastors and church leaders truly do not understand the role of the 5-fold ministry.

Now listen very carefully: If your church has not the functioning of all five of the gifts the Lord gave to build up the church, then your church will not be built right.

Your church will not come into the unity of the faith and to the knowledge of the Son of God. Your church will be unbalanced, lopsided, crippled. Your church will be immature, tossed to and fro in the cunningness of men with every wind of doctrine. You will try every imaginable program – 'Growth' for example, but never be able to come to the fullness of Christ.

Chapter 8

Making Disciples and Preaching the Gospel

Making disciples and preaching the Gospel are two of the ten principles for building a church. They are basic to Christianity, and taught and preached on as much as other subjects though in implementation they are woefully lacking. Obviously, you can't build a church without souls, and yes, preaching the gospel brings forward the souls – but the disciples must go forth and preach the gospel.

As we read in Ephesians chapter 4, the Lord gave apostles, prophets, evangelists, pastors and teachers as gifts to the church to equip or perfect the saints for the work of the ministry, for the edifying – or building up of the body of Christ. The work of the ministry is the preaching of the gospel.

I've spent much of my Christian walk sharing the gospel. Over and over again I have exhorted others in the church to go out and witness with me and all too often I've heard these words in reply, "That's what you have been called to do, but not me."

I am here to refresh our memory. Jesus said to two of his would-be apostles, Peter and Andrew, in Mt.4:19, "Follow me, and I will make you fishers of men." Then in Lk.9:59-60, as Jesus was walking through a village, he spoke to another man and said 'Follow me'. He went on to say to the man, "Let the dead bury their dead, but go thou and preach the kingdom of God."

Before Christ ascended he promised us that we all would receive power when the Holy Ghost came upon us – the power to be witnesses. There are disciples and then there are real disciples. Real disciples are those who obey the commands of the Lord and go forth proclaiming the good news of Jesus Christ.

Less than 3% of all church members have ever gone out to witness, shared the gospel, and led someone in a prayer of salvation, though they are happy to invite or bring someone to church and hope that somebody gets saved in the church.

I've asked countless pastors this question: 'Who is the last member in this church who's here because someone in the congregation went out and led that person to the Lord?' The question most often leaves the person speechless, so you get the picture.

Most of what I'm citing occurs because of a lack of discipleship. To me the most important part of discipleship is hands on training. That's what Jesus did for three years. And that's what the church today is lacking. Most Christians have never been 'discipled' by anyone. That brings us back to the 5-fold ministry and why we need multiple people with experience in sharing the gospel to equip and train the saints.

Most churches will flunk out when it comes to two principles of building the church — making disciples and preaching the gospel. Is your church looking more and more like it's in ruins?

CHAPTER 9

The Role of an Apostle

Are apostles for today?

At least half of all Christians do not believe that the apostolic ministry exists today. For generations Christians have been taught a variety of views, all of which basically deny the existence of apostles today. Most Bible commentaries take this stand on apostles. They have been taught that there were only 13 apostles, Paul being the 13th, and that is where the line ended.

Another teaching is that by the end of the writing of the scriptures, the foundation of the Church had already been laid, and it is sufficient for pastors who can aptly apply the word of God to begin new churches. Both of these concepts are in error.

Only in recent years has the concept of the five-fold ministry surfaced. As Christians have had the opportunity of reading the Bible and studying it, they have discovered the passage in Ephesians 4, which we have been looking at. Clearly, our Lord's appointing of those gifted for the fivefold ministry after his ascension indicates that these men were to operate in their respective offices even today.

Let us look at the progression of apostolic ministry in the Bible. If, in fact, there were other apostles aside from the 13 raised up by our Lord, the fact would indicate that the Lord intended this ministry to continue.

Let's look at what the Bible clearly says about designated apostles. For example, Barnabas: "Which when the apostles, Barnabas and Paul, heard of, they rent their clothes, and ran in among the people, crying out." (Acts 14:14)

And Silas and Timothy: (1 Thes.1:1) "Paul, and Silvanus, and Timotheus, unto the church of the Thessalonians which is in God the Father and in the Lord Jesus Christ: Grace be unto you, and peace, from God our Father, and the Lord Jesus Christ." And 1Thes.2:6, "Nor of men sought we glory, neither of you, nor yet of others, when we might have been burdensome, as the apostles of Christ."

We see Silas and Timothy included together with Paul. Timothy never saw the Lord, he was from Lystra in Turkey. I'm quite confident that other apostles never saw the Lord either. Additional apostles that we find in the New Testament are Apollos, Adronicus and Junias, Titus, and James the Lord's brother.

Yes indeed, apostles are for today! So what is the role or function of an apostle?

Number 1: An apostle is a messenger.

Apostle, from the Greek word Apostolos, means "a

messenger" or "one who is sent." Jesus was an apostle as we learned from Heb.3:1. Jesus was sent forth by the father with a specific message of salvation to a lost world. Jesus extended this apostolic ministry when he chose the Twelve. It is interesting to note that Jesus did not choose 12 pastors, nor 12 teachers or 12 evangelists – nor even 12 prophets to send forth.

He chose 12 disciples, and designated those apostles because the message needed to go forth. I believe that as long as this message of salvation needs to go forth there will still be a need for apostles.

The first priority of an apostle therefore is to act as a messenger. But what exactly is the message to be proclaimed? The answer's in 2Cor.5:17-21: "Therefore if any man be in Christ, he is a new creature: old things are passed away; behold, all things are become new. And all things are of God, who hath reconciled us to himself by Jesus Christ, and hath given to us the ministry of reconciliation; To wit, that God was in Christ, reconciling the world unto himself, not imputing their trespasses unto them; and hath committed unto us the word of reconciliation. Now then we are ambassadors for Christ, as though God did beseech you by us: we pray you in Christ's stead, be ye reconciled to God. For he hath made him to be sin for us, who knew no sin, that we might be made the righteousness of God in him."

The message of a true apostle is the reconciliation of man unto God through Jesus Christ. Paul fine-tuned this message in First Corinthians 15:1-4, as we read earlier, that the gospel of salvation which Paul preached was that Christ died for our sins, was buried, and rose from the dead.

Paul puts forth the death and resurrection of Jesus Christ as of first importance. Here lies the heart of the apostolic ministry. There are those who go forth throughout the world with teachings on many subjects. They are not apostles. There are Christian leaders who have planted multiple churches, but unless the message of the cross has been preached with the subsequent conversion of new souls, then these men were not apostles.

It's not the renting of a building, setting up a coffee shop, having a band play loud music, and advertising your opening that is the mark of an apostle. A give away to someone who is a false apostle is whether they stick around. Do they become the leader of a local church and take in all the glory and the money. True apostles move on. They are compelled by the Spirit to go forth to other places and preach this gospel.

This is now an extremely important issue because so many today claim to be apostles. The church needs to know who the real apostles are.

Let me share two key passages. ICor.4:15, "For though ye have ten thousand instructors in Christ, yet have ye not many fathers: for in Christ Jesus I have begotten you through the gospel."

And 1Cor.9:1-2, "Am I not an apostle? am I not free? have I not seen Jesus Christ our Lord? are not ye my work in the Lord? If I be not an apostle unto others, yet doubtless

I am to you: for the seal of mine apostleship are ye in the Lord."

It's leading many to the Lord through the preaching of the gospel that is the mark and seal of a true apostle.

Number 2: Apostles lay the foundation

This was discussed in our chapter on the "Pattern." Our primary scripture was from Eph.2:19–22 and indicated that apostles and prophets laid the foundation.

The obvious question that arises is, "Why can't pastors lay a foundation?"

The heart of the answer is seen in our passage on the fivefold ministry from Eph.4:7: "But unto every one of us is given grace according to the measure of the gift of Christ."

Jesus is the one who builds a church. He has a divine pattern of which we are to follow in detail. Once there are new converts a foundation needs to be laid. This is an important task upon which the integrity of the whole building will rest. Christ has chosen to gift only a few to lay the foundation – apostles and prophets.

What sets the apostle apart? It is the measure of God's grace given unto him to accomplish this work. Paul said, "According to the grace of God which is given unto me, as a wise masterbuilder, I have laid the foundation, and another buildeth thereon. But let every man take heed how he buildeth thereupon." (1Cor.3:10)

Paul was able to lay the foundation of the church in a unique and powerful way because he was a wise masterbuilder, and he attributed this ability to the grace of God.

Number 3: Apostles equip the saints.

In the previous chapter we saw that two of the principles of building were to make disciples and preach the gospel. Like all those in the fivefold ministry, part of the work is "the perfecting of the saints, for the work of the ministry, for the edifying of the body of Christ." Eph4:12 Do these self-proclaimed apostles have followers as they go out preaching the gospel and healing the sick? Are there miracles that follow? Are they devoted to hands on training as Jesus was?

Number 4: Apostles are involved in church government

'Elders' was the term given those who were the rulers in a church. Peter declared himself an elder in 1Pet.5:1a, "The elders which are among you I exhort, who am also an elder ...."

The apostles Paul and Barnabas appointed elders in each church they established. Acts 14:21-23, "And when they had preached the gospel to that city, and had taught many, they returned again to Lystra, and to Iconium, and Antioch, Confirming the souls of the disciples, and exhorting them to continue in the faith, and that we must through much tribulation enter into the kingdom of God. And when they had ordained them elders in every church, and had prayed with fasting, they commended them to the Lord, on whom they believed."

Thus apostles were not only part of church government,

they appointed the elders. Who better to appoint elders than those who had birthed and fathered those in the church?

Number 5: Apostles bring unity to the church

Our passage about the ministry of apostles, prophets, evangelists, pastors and teachers found in Eph4:7-16 has revealed a treasure of information regarding the building up of the church. All of these gifted men helped to bring a unity of the faith, and a knowledge of the Son of God to the body of Christ so that we are not tossed to and fro by every wind of doctrine.

Many teachings brought into the house of God are half truths and half lies. For example, the church is just about split on the issue of whether a Christian can lose his or her salvation. It's caused havoc in the church. Close Christian friends have parted ways and churches have split over the issue. I'm convinced that the apostle Paul would be able to set us straight. Why? Because apostles have great insight into the word of God.

This was not meant to be an exhaustive study on apostles. Hopefully you begin to get a picture of the life and walk of a true apostle.

CHAPTER 10

The Role of a Prophet

Let me begin this chapter by sharing one verse of scripture from The Book of Revelation. "Notwithstanding I have a few things against thee, because thou sufferest that woman Jezebel, which calleth herself a prophetess, to teach and to seduce my servants to commit fornication, and to eat things sacrificed unto idols." Rev.2:20.

This was part of a letter written to the church at Thyatira. The Lord was irate over this woman Jezebel who proclaimed herself to be a prophetess. He was upset with the church because they allowed her to teach false doctrine that was misleading and corrupting the people at Thyatira. Further, as we read on, if this church did not repent of their ways the Lord was going to cause great tribulation and kill her children with death. Quite a chilling reaction.

I've shared this scripture because this is where I believe the 21ˢᵗ century church is now. In some charismatic circles everyone wants to prophesy and claim to be a prophet. People write down predictions and prophecies they claim are from the Lord which never come to pass. Others prophesy with such a broad scope that it is almost meaningless, and sooner or later their 'prophecies' are almost sure to come to happen.

Churches have accepted such people into their midst with no proof of their office as a prophet, even if they prophecy over the congregation one by one, with little detail, promising each one a blessed future, and then take their donation and leave.

The prophet Micah put it well: "If a man walking in the spirit and falsehood do lie, saying, I will prophesy unto thee of wine and of strong drink; he shall even be the prophet of this people."

Countless pastors now have self-proclaimed themselves to be a prophet with no one in the church to object. This is all an abomination to the Lord and counterproductive to building up the household of God. Yes, there are true prophets today. We just need to find them and allow them to minister in the local church.

So my approach in this chapter is first to answer the question, "How do we recognize a prophet?"

How to recognize a prophet today.

Biblically there are three categories of people when it comes to prophecy. Chapters 12 & 14 of 1Corinthians teach that all Christians can prophecy, and that there are also those who have the gift of prophecy.

And remember that in Eph.4 we learned that a few have been called as a prophet. We want to know who does hold the office of prophet – for we do not want these 'professional' prophesiers.

It's sort of like a man applying for a job. We look at his resume. First, we in the church need to know what the resume of a prophet looks like.

Of first importance to the life of a true prophet is the proclamation of the gospel.

Does the individual have extensive experience in going out to preach? Prophets are disciples first, before becoming a prophet, just as the 12 apostles were. Disciples were trained to preach the kingdom of God. We have already looked at the fact that prophets equip the saints for the work of the ministry – the preaching of the gospel.

They also lay a foundation beginning with Jesus Christ crucified and resurrected. I can't see this happening without hands on experience in sharing the good news. We find in Rev.19:10, "...for the testimony of Jesus is the spirit of prophecy."

Prophets can't help themselves in testifying to the salvation that comes through faith in Christ. This is what will separate most from whether they are a true prophet of the Lord.

Prophets will preach on repentance. The Old Testament prophets did, and John the Baptist preached repentance and so did Jesus.

The prophet Isaiah was called by the Lord to "Go and tell this people." The people of Israel were rebellious, deceitful and unwilling to listen to instruction. They wanted to hear pleasant things: illusions and false prophecies. The people did not want to be confronted with the Holy One and the Word of God. Sound familiar?!

Isaiah hoped they would repent. And the prophet Jonah was sent to Nineveh and preached against it because of its wickedness.

Did any of the prophets speak concerning the household of God? We know the prophet Haggai did, as cited earlier. Here's what the prophet Ezekiel had to say about the household of God in Ezek.43:10-11, "Thou son of man, shew the house to the house of Israel, that they may be ashamed of their iniquities: and let them measure the pattern. And if they be ashamed of all that they have done, shew them the form of the house, and the fashion thereof, and the goings out thereof, and the comings in thereof, and all the forms thereof, and all the ordinances thereof, and all the forms thereof, and all the laws thereof: and write it in their sight, that they may keep the whole form thereof, and all the ordinances thereof, and do them."

These verses speak concerning the pattern and fashion after which the household of God was built, almost exactly the same as the problem that is being brought forth in these pages. It also speaks to the solution – for the solution begins with whether the church will be ashamed of its iniquities by not following the Lord's design in building the church.

Considering that Jesus said he would build the church, it would be hard for me if someone claimed to be a prophet and yet had not received a revelation into the building of the church.

Prophets will prophecy. We can distinguish the real from the false prophet by the little details in the prophecy. Specific and detailed prophecies eliminate the possibility of mere guessing and playing the odds.

A great example comes in the book of Acts chapter 9:10-12: "And there was a certain disciple at Damascus, named Ananias; and to him said the Lord in a vision, Ananias. And he said, Behold, I am here, Lord. And the Lord said unto him, Arise, and go into the street which is called Straight, and enquire in the house of Judas for one called Saul, of Tarsus: for, behold, he prayeth, And hath seen in a vision a man named Ananias coming in, and putting his hand on him, that he might receive his sight."

Here Ananias receives a vision from the Lord concerning the conversion of Saul. The Lord spoke to Ananias in very specific detail. This is why we need to keep records of prophecies to see if they come to pass, the mark of a true prophet.

One characteristic of a prophet will be 'lover of truth.' Prophets hate iniquity, deceitfulness and lies. They will always be on the side of righteousness and defend the poor. Everything is black and white to the prophet. As such, they will be students of the scriptures and able to rightly divide truth from error.

Prophets should be leaders or elders in the local body. In Acts 13:1-3 we read, "Now there were in the church that was at Antioch certain prophets and teachers; as Barnabas, and Simeon that was called Niger, and Lucius of Cyrene, and Manaen, which had been brought up with Herod the tetrarch, and Saul. As they ministered to the Lord, and fasted, the Holy Ghost said, Separate me Barnabas and Saul for the work whereunto I have called them. And when they had fasted and prayed, and laid their hands on them, they sent them away."

It is clear that prophets and teachers were leaders in the church at Antioch. Notice that there is no mention of a 'pastor' as a leader or elder. It is important that prophets, alongside those in the fivefold ministry, be a part of church leadership, and that their gifting is not only expressed but implemented for the sake of the building up of the church.

Prophets should be allowed to speak during the church service. We see this in 1Cor.14 in which the church service is described. Vs 23, "If therefore the whole church be come together into one place…." And verse 29, "Let the prophets speak two or three, and let the other judge."

Prophets may bring forth a word of instruction. Or speak to strengthen, encourage or comfort those in the church. They may expose sin and the need to repent. The issue is, that we need to allow the prophets to speak, and we need to know who the real prophets are, so we are hearing truth the majority of the time.

Lastly I would like to address the belief of many that prophecy has ceased and thus prophets are no longer needed.

This can get quite complicated but let me list some of the more pressing reasons why they still exist today.

1. Number one is that our Lord is still building the church. The church has not reached maturity and thus is still in need of prophets to build up the church.

2. Those who believe prophecy has ceased have been taught with the completion of the Bible that there is no need for 'new' revelation. Those who spoke in the church at Corinth spoke what we call a 'now' word. It was for right now, at this moment, a word to strengthen, encourage or comfort those in attendance. We still need this today. God knows what the people need to hear. All was spoken to build up the people. The prophets may have gotten up and exposed a particular sin that had festered in the congregation. It needed to be rooted out.

3. If prophecy does not exist today then I can make an argument that much of the New Testament no longer applies. So why has it been included? To mislead us? Heavens no! Even Christ spoke concerning prophets and apostles in Matthew 23 and in Revelation.

4. And maybe the most compelling reason prophets exist today comes from 1Cor.13:8-12: "Charity never faileth: but whether there be prophecies, they shall fail; whether there be tongues, they shall cease; whether there be knowledge, it shall vanish away.

For we know in part, and we prophesy in part. But when that which is perfect is come, then that which is in part shall be done away. When I was a child, I spake as a child, I understood as a child, I thought as a child: but when I became a man, I put away childish things. For now we see through a glass, darkly, but then face to face: now I know in part; but then shall I know even as also I am known." Those who speak against prophecy today cite verse 8 and claim that this verse says that the gifts of the Spirit – including prophecy, will cease. They fail to read on to see that this will come to pass when perfection comes, when we will see, (the Lord Jesus Christ), face to face. This obviously won't happen until the Lord returns. My most trusted study Bible advocates that most of the gifts have ceased along with prophecy. But then they come to this one passage and say, "We cannot reconcile our position that the gifts have ceased based on this scripture because it clearly won't occur until the Lord returns."

This by no means has been an exhaustive study on prophets but I hope it has been helpful. I leave you with one main thought: prophets are for today and are vital to the building up of the body of Christ.

CHAPTER 11

Spiritual Gifting of the Saints

As we looked at the ways in which the Lord builds we learned that the Lord provides the pattern and supplies the builders. This led us to Eph4, where the Lord gave men as spiritual gifts – apostles, prophets, evangelists, pastors and teachers – to build up the body of Christ.

The question now becomes, are there others that the Lord gifts to build up the church? The following two passages address that question.

1Cor.12:7-10, "But the manifestation of the Spirit is given to every man to profit withal. For to one is given by the Spirit the word of wisdom; to another the word of knowledge by the same Spirit; To another faith by the same Spirit; to another the gifts of healing by the same Spirit; To another the working of miracles; to another prophecy; to another discerning of spirits; to another divers kinds of tongues; to another the interpretation of tongues:"

Rm.12:6-8, "Having then gifts differing according to the grace that is given to us, whether prophecy, let us prophecy according to the proportion of faith; Or ministry, let us wait on our ministering: or he that teacheth, on teaching; Or he that exhorteth, on exhortation: he that giveth, let him do it with simplicity; he that ruleth, with diligence: he that sheweth mercy, with cheerfulness."

Thus every believer has been given at least one spiritual gift for the common good.

So how do these spiritual giftings benefit everyone? The answer is found in 1Cor.14:3-4, "But he that prophesieth speaketh unto men to edification, and exhortation, and comfort. He that speaketh in a unknown tongue edifieth himself; but he that prophesieth edifieth the church." And in verse 1Cor.14:12, "Even so ye, for as much as ye are zealous of spiritual gifts. Seek that ye may excel to the edifying of the church." Spiritual gifts benefit everyone by building up the church. Remember, we are a spiritual house – and can only be built up spiritually.

Since every believer has a spiritual gift we see the importance of the verses in 1Cor.12:12-26. These verses basically say that the body of Christ is a unit made up of many parts, each part of equal importance, with no part to say to another, 'I don't need you.'

We now see why Paul says in 1Cor.12:1, "Now concerning spiritual gifts, brethren, I would not have you ignorant." He is speaking not just in the sense of what the spiritual gifts are but about the use of them.

Most Christians do not even know what their spiritual gifts are, and those that do are seldom permitted an opportunity to use them. This is where our church service comes in. It is or should be a place/time where every Christian has opportunity to exercise his or her spiritual gifting.

A final point: in the Romans 12 passage above, it is implied that if a man's gift is teaching then let him teach; if a man's gift is ruling, then let him govern. It says – "… let them." These are gifted people whom the Lord puts in a particular body for the purpose of building up that body.

Who are we to oppose the will of God? Local churches should be doing everything they can to allow these gifts to emerge. Unfortunately, these are coveted positions within most local churches, and some pastors prohibit those called by God to minister with their gifting – in direct opposition to the Lord's directions.

The 6th principle in building the church is spiritual gifting.

CHAPTER 12

The Church Service

Here in America every Sunday morning, millions of Christians gather for their weekly service. Many speak of it as their worship service. Maybe because that's what they enjoy the most. We've all grown up attending what I call a traditional service, so we pretty much know what will happen on Sunday in any denominational church we visit. And we can gauge the rest of the day, knowing the service will last no more than an hour or so.

So I have one simple question: How should a church service be run? What should happen during the church service? A novel thought! The obvious follow up question would be, 'Is there any passage in the Bible that would guide us in this matter?"

The answer is yes. Low and behold there is a passage of scripture that speaks of the church service. 1Cor.14:23-32, "If therefore the whole church be come together into one place, and all speak with tongues, and there come in those that are unlearned, or unbelievers, will they not say that ye are mad? But if all prophecy, and there come in one that believeth not, or one unlearned, he is convinced of all, he is judged of all: And thus are the secrets of his heart made manifest; and so falling down on his face he will worship God, and report that God is in you of a truth. How is it then, brethren? When ye come together, every one of you hath a psalm, hath a doctrine, hath a tongue, hath a revelation, hath an interpretation. Let all things be done unto edifying. If any man speak in an unknown tongue, let it be by two, or at the most by three, and that by course; and let one interpret. But if there be no interpreter, let him keep silence in the church; and let him speak to himself, and to God. Let the prophets speak two or three, and let the other judge. If any thing be revealed to another that sitteth by, let the first hold his peace. For ye may all prophecy one by one, that all may learn, and all may be comforted. And the spirits of the prophets are subject to the prophets."

Looks like the church service in Corinth was definitely not boring, and almost assuredly lasted longer than today's typical service. If anyone had a song to sing, they could sing it. They didn't need professional singers, a choir or a band, to be in tune with the Holy Spirit. There were those who spoke in tongues and others interpreted, some prophesied, various people brought forth a word of instruction or a revelation.

Prophets spoke and others would judge the word. This is where spiritual gifts were allowed to function all for the purpose of edification, to build up one another in Christ.

This service was certainly not a one-man show. None of these things that took place in the early church services were optional. At the end of verse 26 we find, "Let all things be done unto edifying." They were commanded per the Apostle Paul's letter to let all these things happen when they came together.

I'm reminded of what Jesus spoke on this matter in Mark 7:9, "And he said unto them, "Full well ye reject the commandment of God, that ye may keep your own tradition."

And sadly, we too have eliminated from our gatherings the workings of the Holy Spirit, as members of the church body are muzzled and not permitted to speak. Some churches cram in two or three services all in one morning – to be sure the folk are out before the football games start.

There is no time to allow individuals the opportunity to exercise their spiritual gifts. I attended a city-wide prayer meeting for revival that closely resembled our passage in 1Cor.14. It was glorious as so many came forward and were allowed to use their gifting. Truly the Lord was in the House.

Let me just add that I find it astounding that when I ask Christians, even pastors, where in the Bible a church service is described, not one (so far as I remember) brought up this passage in 1Cor. 14. Oh if only the church would get focused on the words of Jesus Christ, when he said, 'I will build my church."

Our 7th principle in building the church is 'the church service.'

Chapter 13

Christian Fellowship

The 8th principle in building a church has to do with fellowship. What does fellowship have to do with the edification of a *church*. We find the word *fellowship* right after Peter preached on what we call Pentecost, where it was recorded that three thousand souls were added to the church.

This account is in Acts 2:41-4: "Then they that gladly received his word were baptized: and the same day there were added unto them about three thousand souls. And they continued steadfastly in the apostles' doctrine and fellowship, and in breaking of bread, and in prayers. And fear came upon every soul: and many wonders and signs were done by the apostles. And all that believed were together, and had all things common; And sold their possessions and goods, and parted them to all men, as every man had need. And they continued daily with one accord in the temple, and breaking bread from house to house, did eat their meat with gladness and singleness of heart. Praising God, and having favour with all the people. And the Lord added to the church daily such as should be saved."

The new converts seemed to be meeting almost daily as they devoted themselves to the apostles' doctrine, fellowship, and the breaking of bread and prayer.

A few chapters later in the Book of Acts Peter and John are let out of prison. They go back to where many of the believers were staying and shared what had happened to them, and then it says they lifted up their voice to God "with one accord."

This is how the prayer ended and what followed, Acts 4: 29-32: "And now, Lord, behold their threatening: and grant unto thy servants, that with all boldness they may speak thy word, By stretching forth thine hand to heal; and that signs and wonders may be done by the name of thy holy child Jesus, And when they had prayed, the place was shaken where they were assembled together; and they were all filled with the Holy Ghost, and they spake the word of God with boldness. And the multitude of them that believed were of one heart and of one soul: neither said any of them that ought of the things which he possessed was his own, but they had all things common."

Of note here is that all the believers were of one accord, of one mind and soul, and they prayed that they all would be emboldened to preach the gospel. The result was the place where they were meeting was shaken and they all spoke the word of God boldly.

And one more verse, Phil.1:27, "Only let your

conversation be as it becometh the gospel of Christ: that whether I come and see you, or else be absent, I may hear of your affairs, that ye stand fast in one spirit, with one mind striving together for the faith of the gospel;" The conversation in Christian fellowship should be that which becometh the gospel of Jesus Christ. Christian fellowship is where Christians can become united to one another by common beliefs, purposes and goals that center around the gospel of Christ.

It would be hard not to believe that in the cited scriptures much of the conversation amongst the believers was about those who just got saved. The importance of true Christian fellowship is that it reinforces these things in our mind and helps us to focus on Christ and his desires for us. As iron sharpens iron, Christian fellowship sharpens our faith and our willingness to exercise our faith. Christian fellowship is also a place where the spiritual gifting of more mature Christians can be exercised to edify, exhort and comfort the newer converts.

We can also see how apostles were used to set the example when Christians gathered in the early church. It should be no different today. Christian fellowship is hugely important in the life of any church. It permits someone who has just been saved to grow and mature spiritually and be built up in Christ Jesus.

This is our 8th principle in building up the church: "Christian fellowship."

The fellowship that exists in a local church is a direct reflection of where that church stands spiritually – with the Lord. It's simple. It revolves around the matter of Christian conversation. In 2ⁿᵈ Corinthians chapter 5, Paul says, "if any man be in Christ, he is a new creature: old things are passed away: behold all things are become new."

When we accept Christ as our Lord and Saviour, our life style should change.

Our conversation should change. We are told, "Be ye not equally yoked with unbelievers, for what fellowship hath righteousness with unrightousness? And what communion hath light with darkness?" 2Cor.6:14.

Our citizenship is in heaven. Our minds and conversations are to be on heavenly things, not earthly things.

For some 40 years, I have been in the church and been invited to an untold number of churches and their fellowships. Most of those I would never go back to. Why? Because they are so worldly. They love to eat, oh do they love to eat! And all the while, their conversation is on earthly things. They speak about sports, football, their latest golf outing, the problems at work or finding work, their vacation, troubles with family and friends, health issues – and on and on and on it goes. No one, and I mean no one, ever mentions leading someone to the Lord or how the Lord spoke to them, or what the Lord is doing in their own life.

This is disgraceful, and in no way resembles Christian fellowship.

So, speaking truthfully, I must say these are dead churches. They are not new creations in Christ. What a sad way to end this chapter.

So what can these churches do? Why, they must go back to preaching the gospel. And to building the church.

CHAPTER 14

Church Government

After speaking and leading many seminars on Building the Church, I am convinced that the most important principle for building the church relates to church government. In every seminar I've led, the church leadership agreed that the 10 principles I present are biblical and of huge importance.

They also agreed that they are doing less than 20% and do have a desire to utilize the 10 principles. And yet, astonishingly, nothing ever seems to get done. Why? Well, pure and simple, it comes back to church government.

Church government, as we shall soon see, is made up of elders who are to rule over the local church. They are the ones who direct the affairs of the church. Thus, whether your church will seek out apostles, prophets and evangelists to help build the church depends on the rulers (church government).

Whether your church will follow the church service as outlined in 1Cor.14 – and also allow spiritual gifts again, goes back to your rulers. Whether your church will diligently seek to make disciples and go out and preach the gospel is also dependent on the elders.

So how should a church be governed? Below is a list of 10 biblical passages that make it easy to determine how every local church should be governed.

I've numbered the scriptures 1–10, so as to refer to them later.

1. Acts 13:1-3 "Now there were in the church that was at Antioch certain prophets and teachers; as Barnabas, and Simeon that was called Niger, and Lucius of Cyrene, and Manaen, which had been brought up with Herod the tetrarch, and Saul. As they ministered to the Lord, and fasted, the Holy Ghost said, Separate me Barnabas and Saul for the work whereunto I have called them. And when they had fasted and prayed, and laid their hands on them, they sent them away."

2. Acts 14:14a, 23 "Which when the apostles, Barnabas and Paul ...." and verse 23 "And when they had ordained them elders in every church, and had prayed with fasting, they commended them to the Lord, on whom they believed."

3. Acts 20:17, 28 "And from Miletus he sent to Ephesus, and called the elders of the church." And verse 28 "Take heed therefore unto yourselves, and to all the flock, over the which the Holy Ghost hath made you overseers, to feed the church of God, which he hath purchased with his own blood."

4. Phil. 1:1 "Paul and Timotheus, the servants of Jesus Christ, to all the saints in Christ Jesus which are at Philippi, with the bishops and deacons…"

5. Eph. 4:11-12 "And he gave some, apostles; and some, prophets; and some, evangelists; and some pastors and teachers; for the perfecting of the saints, for the work of the ministry, for the edifying of the body of Christ…"

6. 1 Tim. 3:1, 2 "This is a true saying, If a man desire the office of a bishop, he desireth a good work. A bishop then must be blameless, the husband of but one wife, vigilant, sober, of good behaviour, given to hospitality, apt to teach;"

7. 1 Tim. 5:17 "Let the elders that rule well be counted worthy of double honour, especially they who labour in the word and doctrine."

8. Titus 1:5 "For this cause I left thee in Crete, that thou shouldest set in order the things that are wanting, and ordain elders in every city, as I had appointed thee:"

9. 1 Pet. 5:1-4 "The elders which are among you I exhort, who am also an elder, and a witness of the sufferings of Christ, and also a partaker of the glory that shall be revealed: Feed the flock of God which is among you, taking the oversight thereof, not by constraint, but willingly; not for filthy lucre, but of a ready mind; Neither as being lords over God's heritage, but being ensamples to the flock.

And when the chief Shepherd shall appear, ye shall receive a crown of glory that fadeth not away."

10. 3 John 1, and 9-10 " The elder unto the well beloved Gaius, whom I love in the truth... I wrote unto the church: but Diotrephes, who loveth to have the preeminence among them, receiveth us not. Wherefore, if I come, I will remember his deeds which he doeth, prating against us with malicious words: and not content therewith, neither doth he himself receive the brethren, and forbiddeth them that would, and casteth them out of the church."

From these scriptures, we find five basic principles or rules to determine how a church should be governed.

Rule 1: There are three distinct groups of people in the church: bishops (overseers in NIV), deacons, and saints.

Refer to scripture 4

1Tim. 3:1, 8 confirms this by speaking of the requirements to be a bishop (overseer) or deacon.

Rule 2: The leaders of the church are bishops (overseers), referring to the office, or elder (shepherds), referring to the man.

Refer to scriptures 2, 3, 6-9

In every church that the apostle Paul established it says that he appointed elders over the local church. "Elders" is the correct terminology for church leaders. Nowhere does the New Testament refer to a pastor as the head of a church or to a system of pastors to rule.

Rule 3: There are always multiple elders in every local church.

Refer to scriptures 2, 3, 7-9

Throughout the New Testament leaders are always referred to in the plural. There were multiple elders who preached and taught the word who were worthy of double honour. Further, it would seem from 1Tim. 3:1-2 that anyone who desires to be an elder and meets the criteria as outlined in 1 Timothy should be so ordained. Having additional credentials should not be a requisite.

Rule 4: Elders have equal authority. There was never a head or chief elder.

Refer to scriptures 7, 9, 10.

Never is the term bishop or pastor used in the scriptures to denote a position superior to an elder. Nowhere in the New Testament is there mention of a 'senior' pastor or implication that one pastor has greater authority than the other pastors. Even Peter proclaimed himself to be just a fellow elder and emphasized that there was only one Chief Shepherd – the Lord Jesus Christ. It is man who established hierarchies in the institutional church system. God did not ordain them. It all began with Diotrephes and the love for preeminence.

Rule 5: Elders were comprised of apostles, prophets, evangelists, teachers and shepherds.

Refer to scriptures 1, 5, 7, 9, 10.

Very clearly we can see from Acts 13:1-3 that prophets and teachers were involved in the decision making in the church at Antioch. So were Barnabas and Saul who were to become apostles. Since all these gifted men of the 5-fold ministry were gifts given by the Lord to build the church and equip the saints it would seem obvious they all should be involved in the preaching and teaching and decision making. Each should have equal access to the pulpit. Having multiple elders with equal authority who are knowledgeable in and committed to the scriptures prevents a church from indulging, or investing in, worthless programs while neglecting the great commission and the making of disciples.

The professing church government of today is founded upon unbiblical principles. It is a monarchy where man rules instead of a theocracy where God rules, thus rejecting Jesus as King. This monarchy is where you have only one pastor as the ruler or where you have a 'senior' pastor or 'lead' pastor who dominates over other pastors or a board and makes the final decision. It is evil and an abomination to the Lord. It is in error and it is a sin to God.

This ungodly church government system has become firmly rooted in Christendom. It has dethroned Jesus as Lord and set man in his place. The pastor has become a god unto the people whether wittingly or unwittingly. With an ungodly government in place every practice, teaching and effort of the saints is adversely affected.

For Jesus to be truly Lord and Christ in your local church, only the government that the Lord instituted through the scriptures can be appropriated.

The Clergy-Laity System

The term clergy-laity goes back to the earliest days of the church. It's a term still around today that divides the saints into two categories of people, the professional and the non-professional. It designates those who are credentialed and scholarly from those who are not, from those who minister and those who don't. In most cases it's the pastors and then everyone else.

No where in the Bible do we see the term clergy or laity. So how then did this teaching originate? It goes back to Diotrephes and his desire for preeminence, to be the leader. Refer back to #10 above – 1John3:9-10. Diotrephes usurped control by becoming the monarchial Bishop presiding over the other elders. He then prohibited others in the church, namely apostles and prophets with authority to correct his lust for power from attending "his" church. This lust for power continued as church leaders separated themselves from the other believers by declaring that they alone could preside over the church service, baptisms, communion and the collections of money. In time, the monarchial bishops became known as priests as only they, like in the Old Testament priests, could minister before the Lord. A huge gulf developed between the priests and other saints which became known as the clergy-laity system.

In the days of Martin Luther and the Protestant Reformation in the 16th century, the Protestants began to use the term pastor rather than priest, and thus it is the pastor who now has become the monarchial bishop.

This clergy-laity system elevates and thereby exalts those who are priests, pastors, bishops or any other church leaders whereby they perform certain functions in the church while diminishing the authority of the other saints. For example, in most churches, only those with certain credentials can preach. The pulpit has become a sacred place for the clergy alone, not for the lowly saint. It is a place for the scholarly and well-learned and not for the uneducated. However, Acts 4:13 says that the Jewish leaders took note of Peter and John and realized that they were unschooled ordinary men, who had been with Jesus. I say give me a message from someone who has been with Jesus and under the power of the Holy Spirit.

Do we know who "these" people are in our church? Or do we just not care because they do not meet our requirements of having a certain academic degree? How sad!

Yet the Bible teaches that we are all priests, members of a royal priesthood, (1 Pet. 2:9). According to 1Corinthians 12 and 14, every Christian has a spiritual gift for the important purpose of building one another up. In the church service, if a brother in the Lord is prompted by the Holy Spirit to sing a song, give a message or share a revelation, then he should to be able to do so to strengthen the body of Christ. God has not changed.

Today each believer not only has the privilege to speak but an obligation to the Lord to use his or her gifts. At stake is the building up of the body of Christ. That's why this 'concept of build' is so very important.

To allow this clergy-laity system to exist is an evil and wicked practice in direct conflict with the will of God to build his church. This system is the invention of men – and is an affront to the glory of God. It has done incalculable harm to the building up of the church.

Church government, the appointing of multiple elders – this is the 9th principle in building the church.

CHAPTER 15

The Poor and the Needy

Principle #10 in building the church is to help the poor and needy. Please take a few moments to read the following scriptures.

Dt. 15:4, "Save when there shall be no more poor among you; for the Lord shall greatly bless thee in the land which the Lord thy God giveth thee for an inheritance to possess it:"

Jer.22:15-16, "Shalt thou reign, because thou closest thyself in cedar? Did not thy father eat and drink, and do judgment and justice, and then it was well with him? He judged the cause of the poor and needy; then it was well with him: was not this to know me? saith the Lord."

Gal.2:9-10, "And when James, Cephas, and John, who seemed to be pillars, perceived the grace that was given unto me and Barnabas the right hands of fellowship; that we should go unto the heathen, and they unto the circumcision. Only they would that we should remember the poor, the same which I also was forward to do."

And one more passage from the early church:

Acts 2:44-45, "And all that believed were together, and had all things common; And sold their possessions and goods, and parted them to all men, as every man had need."

Thank you for reading these. Amidst all the work of applying these 10 principles to building a church, make it a priority to remember the poor and the needy – that it may go well with you as you build God's House.

CHAPTER 16

Show them the Form of the House

In this chapter we will apply the 10 principles of building a church and show how they fit together. First off, we go back and read again a passage in Ezekiel.

Ezek.43:9-10: "Thou son of man, shew the house to the house of Israel, that they may be ashamed of their iniquities: and let them measure the pattern. And if they be ashamed of all that they have done, shew them the form of the house, and the fashion thereof, and the goings out thereof, and the comings in thereof, and all the forms thereof, and all the ordinances thereof, and all the forms thereof, and all the laws thereof, and write it in their sight, that they might keep the whole form thereof, and all the ordinances thereof, and do them."

My mandate is to show the form of the house to the saints.

To those who would pursue building a church according to the Lord's design, I ask "Are they ashamed of their iniquities? Are they ashamed of their sin? Are they ashamed and able to admit that they, man, have been building the church and not the Lord? Will they pick and choose what they feel comfortable changing, or will they build according to the whole form shown them?

Here is a summary of the 10 principles already discussed in this text:

1. Laying the foundation
2. Building upon the foundation
3. The builders of the church – apostles, prophets, evangelists, pastors and teachers
4. Making disciples
5. Preaching the gospel
6. Spiritual gifting of the saints
7. The church service
8. Church fellowship
9. Church government – the appointing of elders
10. Helping the poor and needy

Now let's attempt to put these 10 principles of building the church in some sort of order – or design. To build a church you need people, souls, saints, and therefore the first step in building the church is going out and preaching the gospel.

Go prayerfully, and the Lord will bless you with new converts for building a church. Then what? The next four pages show flowcharts that describe biblically what needs to take place.

The first flowchart gives an overall perspective of what

needs to occur from the beginning of starting a church. Once you have new converts there are three basic things that need to occur:

(1) The laying of a foundation.
(2) Making disciples
(3) Church functions.

The next three flowcharts give the details of these three.

First, a few comments. Recognizing and implementing all those in the 5-fold ministry may be your biggest challenge. In the beginning stages, apostles and prophets should be at the forefront – as we see in the establishment of the church at Antioch in Acts 11:19-26.

I cannot stress enough the need for the correct form of church government, for it is the local church government that will determine if these biblical principles of building will continue to be applied.

And one last point: If God be with you, expect the miraculous.

A church of power is emerging, and it will be the manifestation of the power of God in the name of Jesus Christ that will separate this church from other churches.

May God be with you and bless you, in Jesus' name.

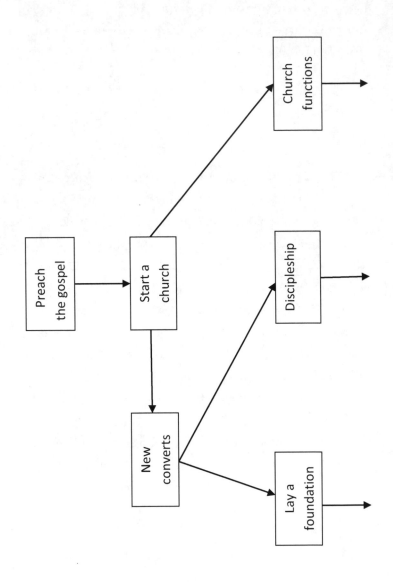

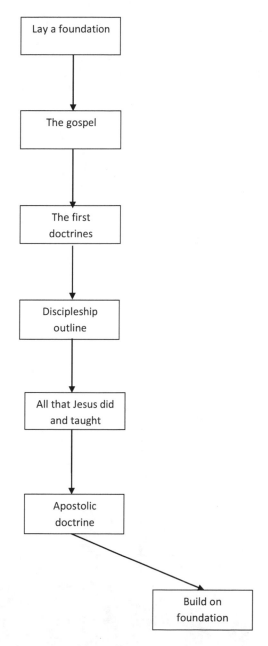

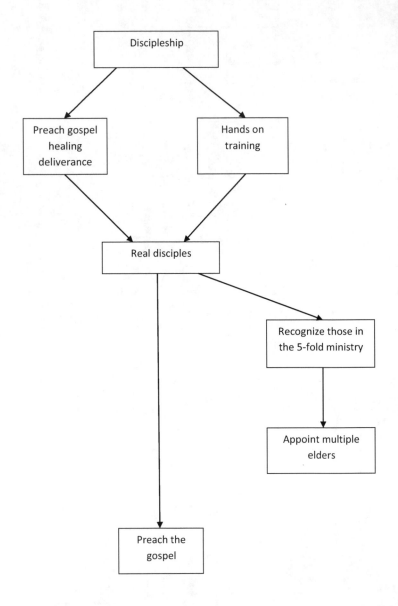

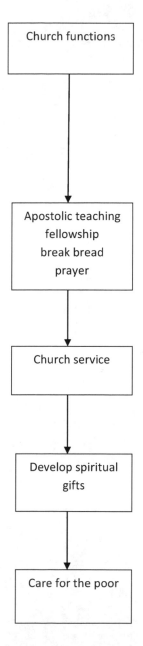

EPILOGUE

It is hoped that this book has been a challenge and blessing to you. Where do we go from here that we may work together to advance the kingdom of God?

If you have any questions feel free to correspond.

Email – donfaix@aol.com

You can call Don Faix at 704–699–6091,

Or write to: Don Faix, 705 Woodbrook Pl. Concord N.C. 28025

Printed in the United States
by Baker & Taylor Publisher Services